THE AMERICAN SOUTHWEST

A GUIDE TO THE WIDE OPEN SPACES

by

NATT N. DODGE

Regional Naturalist, National Park Service

and

HERBERT S. ZIM, Ph.D.

Professor of Education, University of Illinois

ILLUSTRATIONS BY
ARCH AND MIRIAM HURFORD

W9-AUT-469

NEW MEXICO MINERALS DISTRIB.
11003 CENTRAL, NE—HY 66 E.
P. O. BOX 8262 — STA. C
ALBUQUERQUE, NEW MEXICO

SIMO   W YORK

FOREWORD

Everyone knows where the Southwest is, but no two people agree as to what it includes. This book, the first of the Golden Regional Guides, presents to the vacationer, traveler, or interested reader some of the many facets of this appealing land of deserts, mountains, people, places, and events—the Southwest. The book is a guide to the animate and inanimate features of the region, with emphasis on those things most visitors can see and do. It includes sightseeing suggestions, traveling directions, prehistory, history, natural history, Indian lore, and sources of additional information. It is an introduction to the Southwest—one, we hope, that will tempt you to explore further.

Many people have helped in gathering and checking the information in this book. The authors express their grateful thanks to all, especially to Herbert Evison, Sallie Van Valkenburg, Hugh Miller, Bennett Gale, Myrl Walker, and Erik Reed of the National Park Service; and to Stanley Stubbs, Marjory Lambert, and Bertha Dutton of the Laboratory of Anthropology, Santa Fe. Our special thanks are due to Donald Hoffmeister, Hobart Smith, Ira Gabrielson, Alexander Martin, Raymond Carlson, Ray E. Pond, William Carr, and the staff of the Museum of New Mexico. The artists, Arch and Miriam Hurford, have made a rich graphic contribution.

N.N.D.
H.S.Z.

Copyright 1955 by Simon and Schuster, Inc., and Artists and Writers Guild, Inc. All rights reserved, including the right of reproduction in whole or in part in any form. Designed and produced by The Sandpiper Press and Artists and Writers Guild, Inc. Printed in the U.S.A. by Western Printing and Lithographing Company. Published by Simon and Schuster, Inc., Rockefeller Center New York 20, N. Y. Published simultaneously in Canada by The Musson Book Company, Ltd., Toronto.

CONTENTS

Shalako at Zuni Winter Ceremony

MEET THE SOUTHWEST

THE COUNTRY   The Southwest is a region without definite boundaries. Aridity is its principal over-all characteristic. But the region offers amazing contrasts and diversity of climate, geography, and people. Its 465,000 sq. mi. involve nine states and include such superlatives as the lowest land, the biggest canyon, the highest mountain, the driest deserts, the hottest valley, the richest mines, and the oldest towns in the United States. The Southwest is big. But it is also friendly, hospitable, fascinating to live in—full of pleasant surprises, enough for a lifetime.

THE PEOPLE   Newcomers have been drifting into the Southwest for 25,000 years, and the tide is undiminished. According to the 1930 Census, the region had then a population of 1,568,200. By 1950 the number had risen to 2,575,250. These figures do not include the hundreds of thousands of summer tourists and winter vacationers, who come for the clear air, sunshine, and unspoiled scenery.

Mt. Whitney, Calif., 14,495
Mt. Elbert, Colo., 14,431
Mt. Massive, Colo., 14,418
Mt. Harvard, Colo., 14,399
Mt. Blanca, Colo., 14,390
La Plata Peak, Colo., 14,340

The Southwest's Highest Mountains

LAND FORMS Except for the eastern plains portion, there is probably no part of the Southwest from which mountains cannot be seen on a clear day. Mountains rise from desert lowlands and from higher plateaus. Much of the Great Basin Desert is located on plateaulands at elevations of 3,000 to 6,000 ft. A wide tongue of the Rocky Mountains extends deep into the Southwest. Many of the low mountain ranges to the south are as much desert as the lowlands that surround them. Other, higher mountains are green forested islands in a "sea" of desert. The map outlines the major topographic areas of the Southwest.

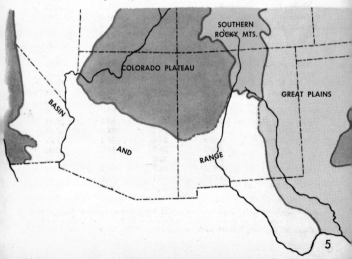

SOUTHERN ROCKY MTS.

COLORADO PLATEAU

GREAT PLAINS

BASIN

AND

RANGE

CLIMATE in this land is dry, warm, and breezy. A clear atmosphere, abundant sunshine, and low humidity are typical. Annual precipitation (rain and snow) varies from 1 to 6 in. in the deserts to 30 to 35 in. in the mountains. Much of the moisture falls as spotty but heavy summer thundershowers or as slow winter soakers. Temperatures generally are moderate but vary with latitude, altitude, and other factors. The low south and west parts of the region are hot and dry, the central plateaulands warm and dry, and the mountains cool and moderately moist. Nights are cool. Winter temperatures are cool to cold, depending upon location. Prevailing winds are from the southwest. "Dusters" are common, but tornadoes are practically unknown.

CLIMATIC DATA

City	Elevation, ft.	Avg. Jan. Temp., deg. F.	Avg. July Temp., deg. F.	Avg. Annual Rainfall, inches
Del Rio, Tex.	948	51.9	84.7	18.58
Lubbock, Tex.	3,195	38.8	79.3	18.89
El Paso, Tex.	3,710	43.4	81.3	7.83
Amarillo, Tex.	3,672	35.3	77.8	21.12
Dodge City, Kan.	2,509	30.3	79.9	20.51
Pueblo, Colo.	4,690	29.4	74.9	11.87
Alamosa, Colo.	7,531	16.9	64.1	6.23
Grand Junction, Colo.	4,583	24.0	78.2	9.06
Raton, N. Mex.	6,666	26.2	68.6	15.42
Roswell, N. Mex.	3,600	39.6	79.0	12.07
Albuquerque, N. Mex.	4,943	33.7	79.0	8.68
Winslow, Ariz.	4,856	32.4	77.2	7.83
Phoenix, Ariz.	1,083	49.7	90.1	7.12
Flagstaff, Ariz.	6,894	25.3	65.2	18.47
Yuma, Ariz.	150	55.3	94.6	3.39
Blanding, Utah	6,075	26.6	72.3	12.77
Milford, Utah	4,962	23.8	74.0	8.44
Ely, Nev.	6,000	23.0	68.4	10.52
Las Vegas, Nev.	2,033	44.2	90.5	4.35
Tonopah, Nev.	6 090	30.1	74.6	4.81
Death Valley, Calif.	152	52.0	101.8	2.17

In the Southwest, temperature variations have been recorded from above 130°F. in summer in Death Valley to below —50°F. in the high mountain valleys of southern Colorado in winter.

LASTING IMPRESSIONS   Despite the bigness of the
Southwest, little things—sights, sounds, and smells—often
create the most lasting impressions. Here are some:

Strings of scarlet chili drying against adobe walls.

Golden aspens mantling a mountain's shoulders.

Lithe relaxation of Navajos outside a trading post.

Awkward speed of a fleeing roadrunner.

Massive thunderhead dragging its braids of rain.

Immobility of tumbleweeds banked against a fence.

Line of resigned autos waiting out a flash flood.

Single-file string of steers approaching a waterhole.

Echoes and silences in a great cliff-dwelling ruin.

Bawling of restless cattle at a roundup.

Heady aroma of campfire coffee.

Carefree boys "in the raw" splashing in a stock tank.

Squeal of a fighting, bucking horse at a rodeo.

Wail of a coyote—and yapping of others—at night.

Drum throbs and shrill chant of an Indian dance.

Musty odor of creosote bush after rain.

Bray of a distant wild burro just after sunrise.

Harsh smell of singed flesh at a branding corral.

Sudden pelting rush of a summer thunderstorm.

Unbelievable immensity of the Grand Canyon.

Juiciness of thick steak broiled over mesquite coals.

Stars that you can reach from your sleeping bag.

Splash and tug of a mountain trout hitting your fly.

Tang of enchiladas smothered in chili sauce.

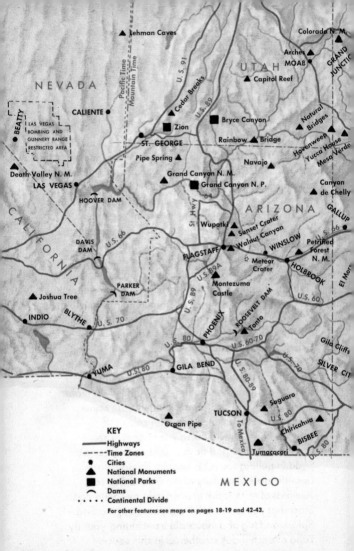

THE MODERN SOUTHWEST

COLORADO

KANSAS

U.S. 40

▲ Black Canyon

U.S. 85

U.S. 50

PUEBLO

U.S. 50

Great
Sand
Dunes

JOHN MARTIN DAM

U.S. 87

U.S. 350

U.S. 160

● DURANGO

ALAMOSA

U.S. 285

OKLAHOMA

Aztec Ruins

▲ Capulin Mountain

U.S. 64

Chaco Canyon ▲

● TAOS

U.S. 64-87

LOS ALAMOS ●
Bandelier ▲

U.S. 85

SANTA FE ●

NEW

TUCUMCARI ●

AMARILLO ●

U.S. 66

● ALBUQUERQUE

U.S. 66

U.S. 60

U.S. 285

U.S. 60

TEXAS

MEXICO

▲ Gran
Quivira

U.S. 70

Mountain Time
Central Time

● LUBBOCK

U.S. 70

ELEPHANT BUTTE
DAM

U.S. 285

ROSWELL ●

U.S. 85

CABALLO
DAM

▲

● ALAMOGORDO

AVALON DAM

White Sands

U.S. 285

● CARLSBAD

U.S. 87

U.S. 70-80

■ Carlsbad Caverns

● MIDLAND

U.S. 80

● EL PASO

RED BLUFF
DAM

U.S. 80

U.S. 290

● ALPINE

0   30   60   90   120

miles

U.S. 90

Big Bend ■

Check Your Route

PLAN YOUR TRIP Begin by studying highway maps and pamphlets obtained from railroads, bus and air lines, travel bureaus, chambers of commerce, and state and federal agencies (see p. 120).

Auto travelers may obtain tour-aid service from the larger gasoline companies. Much of the Southwest is accessible by paved roads, and modern accommodations are available in most towns. During the heavy summer travel season, try to make overnight reservations in advance or stop early to get a better choice. Obey safety rules and highway signs. If you pull a trailer, find out what hills are ahead.

Off the main roads are Indian villages, spectacular scenery, challenging fishing streams. Be careful never to stop for the night in the bottom of a wash or gully; flash floods give no warning. Keep your gas tank at least half full. When off mapped roads, inquire at each opportunity regarding your route and the condition of the road ahead. If you plan to travel back roads, come well equipped. Use the check lists below.

Car Needs	**Your Needs**	
Good spare tire	Canteen of water	Canned foods
Good jack	Gasoline lantern	Matches
Basic tool kit	Flashlight and	First-aid kit
Reserve water for radiator	batteries	Snakebite kit
Reserve gasoline	Kettle or cooking kit	Pocket knife
Ax and shovel	Gasoline stove	Lip-chap stick
Tire pump and patches	"White" gasoline for	Sunglasses
Spare fan belt	stove and lantern	Sunburn lotion
Tire chains	Frying pan	Compass
Towrope	Sturdy hiking shoes	Ball of string
	Wide-brimmed hat	Blankets or sleeping
	Tarpaulin	bag

Camping Locations Are Available in Many Areas

LEAVE THE COUNTRY GREEN AND CLEAN It's good travel manners to enjoy flowers—and leave them for others. Leave all wild animals alone; and keep an eye open for rattlesnakes and scorpions. Don't deface signs, buildings, or natural features. Keep all trash in a paper bag until you drop it into a refuse container or bury it. Always leave a *CLEAN* camp and a *DEAD* fire.

Indians are a proud though friendly people; don't stare or point at them, enter their homes uninvited, or haggle over prices. If you want souvenirs, buy something typical from them or at a trading post.

Help travelers in distress but avoid hitchhikers.

Before starting a hike remember that distances in the Southwest may fool you. Objects appear closer than they are, because of the clean, dry air.

If your car gets stuck in sand, reduce the pressure in your tires to half for better traction.

National parks and monuments are always "open," although accommodations may sometimes be closed. Camping locations are provided in most national forests, in many state and national parks and monuments, and in some state and federal wildlife refuges. Locate campgrounds in advance by referring to p. 120 and to THE CAMPGROUND GUIDE (R. O. Klotz, Campgrounds Unlimited, Blue Rapids, Kan., 1955).

Be careful with fire!

Ghost Town–White Oaks, N. Mex.

DUDE RANCHES AND GHOST TOWNS

Guest or "dude" ranches offer a unique, informal vacation in "back country" close to nature. Some are cattle ranches that take in a few paying guests; others may be swank resorts with swimming pools, cocktail bars, and flashy "cowboys" hired as vocalists. Dude ranches specialize in horseback riding, outdoor cooking, and informal rodeos in which guests may participate. Write to chambers of commerce in Southwest cities for information.

Ghost towns usually are mining camps that have "played out." In some, a few families remain, with perhaps a general store and filling station. Others are completely deserted, in ruins, and difficult to find. Check locally for directions and conditions of roads.

Some ghost towns and dates they were founded:

Southeast California: Panamint City 1861, Calico 1881, Bodie 1859.

Southeast Nevada: Tonopah 1864, Searchlight 1897, Nelson 1860, Bullfrog 1905, Rhyolite 1904, Goldfield 1902, Eldorado Canyon 1875, Blackhorse 1900, Alunite 1875, Aurora 1860.

Southern Colorado: Silverton 1873, Creede 1889, Lake City 1874, Eureka 1876, Animas Forks 1875, White Cross 1876, Alpine 1872, St. Elmos 1879, Romley 1870, Hancock 1880, Sherman 1877, Cunningham Gulch 1874, Victor 1891, Burrows Park 1873.

New Mexico: Kelly 1880, Golden 1839, Dolores 1828, San Pedro 1832, White Oaks 1850, Hillsboro 1877, Mogollon 1889, Elizabeth 1868, Kingston 1880, Tyrone, Gold Dust 1879, Shakespeare.

Arizona: Charleston 1879, Contention City 1879, Tubac 1752, Gila City 1858, Oatman 1900, Tombstone 1877, Jerome 1870, Octave 1862, Hardyville 1856, Stanton 1863, Weaver 1862, Goldroad 1863, Silver King 1875, White Hills 1892, McMillanville 1876, Pinal 1875.

For more about ghost towns read: *The Bonanza Trail,* Muriel S. Wolle, Indiana Univ. Press, Bloomington, 1953.

CALENDAR OF EVENTS

(Verify dates locally.)

January—Jan. 6, Buffalo, Deer, and Eagle Dances at Rio Grande pueblos with installation of pueblo governors. Day of Epiphany, Three Kings Feast in Spanish-American villages. Jan. 23, dances, both plazas, San Ildefonso, N. Mex. Bean, Buffalo, and social dances, Hopi villages.

February—Open golf championships, Phoenix and Tucson, Ariz. Spring training, southern Arizona, for major-league ball teams. Cactus show, Desert Botanical Gardens, Tempe, Ariz. Silver Spur Rodeo, Yuma, Ariz.; Fiesta de los Vaqueros (rodeo). Tucson. Plains Indian dances, Taos, N. Mex. Deer and Buffalo dances at Rio Grande pueblos.

March—Stock show, rodeo, San Angelo and El Paso, Tex. Dons' trek to Superstition Mts. and World's Championship Rodeo, Phoenix; Rawhide Roundup, Mesa, Ariz. Indian dances, Keresan pueblos, N. Mex.

March-April—Easter sunrise services, Grand Canyon and Death Valley, Calif. Yaqui Indian ceremonials, Pascua, near Tucson.

April—Rodeo, Douglas, Ariz.; Ride of Desert Caballeros, Wickenburg, Ariz. Festival of Fine Arts, Tucson. Annual Playday, White Sands, N. Mex.; Desert Cavalcade, Calexico, Calif. Many Green Corn Dances.

May—May 5, Cinco de Mayo (Mexican Independence Day) celebrations, both sides international boundary. Ute Bear Dance, Ignacio, Colo. Ceremonial dances, Taos Pueblo, Corn Dance, Cochiti Pueblo. May 15, Feast of San Ysedro in many Spanish-American towns.

June—Cotton Carnival, Lubbock, Tex. New Mex. Musical Festival, Raton. Dances at Taos, San Juan, Santa Clara, San Ildefonso, and Cochiti Pueblos, N. Mex. Ute Sun Dance, Towaoc, Colo.

July—Frontier Days, Prescott, Ariz.; Annual Rodeo, Silver City, N. Mex. Apache Maidens' Fiesta, Mescalero, N. Mex. All-Tribes Pow-Wow and Hopi Craftsman Exhibit, Flagstaff, Ariz. Rodeo de Santa Fe, N. Mex. July 24, Mormon Pioneer Day celebrations throughout Utah.

August—Inter-Tribal Indian Ceremonials, Gallup, N. Mex. Hopi Snake Dances, Outboard Regatta, Lake Mead, Ariz.-Nev. Apache dances and rodeo, Ruidoso, N. Mex. Corn Dances at several N. Mex. pueblos.

September—Labor Day week-end Fiesta, Santa Fe. New Mexico State Fair, Albuquerque. Indian Rodeo, Winslow, Ariz.; Pima Fiesta and Rodeo, Sacaton, Ariz. Harvest dances at Rio Grande pueblos.

October—Navajo Fair and Rodeo, Shiprock, N. Mex. Apache Autumn Festival, San Carlos, Ariz. Papago Arts and Crafts Exhibit, Sells, Ariz. Oct. 31-Nov. 2, ceremonials at most Rio Grande pueblos.

November—Arizona State Fair, Phoenix. Harvest dances in various Hopi villages, Ariz. Encampment of Death Valley 49'ers, California.

November-December—Famous Shalako ceremonials, Zuni Pueblo, N. Mex. Navajo Mt. Way and Night Way ceremonies on reservation.

December—Dec. 12, Nuestra Señora de Guadalupe ceremonials in many Spanish-American villages. Dec. 24-30, Christmas lighting and processions at many Spanish-American villages and Indian pueblos.

KEY:

— 1-week tour
— 2-week tour (summer)
— 2-week tour (winter)
— 3-week tour
● Cities
○ National Parks and Monuments

FOUR TOURS

ONE-WEEK TOUR This automobile tour through the heart of the Southwest may be taken in any season; April or October is most comfortable. You can work out other routes from the next two pages or pp. 120-156. Study maps and literature each evening.

First Day: Tour Carlsbad Caverns (4 hours). On to El Paso, Tex., and spend the evening across the border in Juárez, Mexico.

Second Day: It's a day's drive on U.S. 80 to Tucson, Ariz., but you'll have time to see the open-pit mine at Bisbee and stop at old Tombstone.

Third Day: See San Xavier Mission and the Arizona-Sonora Desert Museum near Tucson. Stop at Casa Grande Nat. Mon. and Desert Botanical Gardens near Tempe. Night in Phoenix.

Fourth Day: Take the Oak Creek Canyon branch of U.S. 89, visiting the Jerome Mine Museum, Tuzigoot Ruin, and Montezuma Castle Cliff Dwelling on the way to Flagstaff, Ariz.

Fifth Day: On to Grand Canyon, via Williams. Take the West Rim Drive before lunch, leaving by way of Desert View and Cameron. You can stop at a couple of trading posts, see Sunset Crater, and still reach Winslow in time for supper.

Sixth Day: Take U.S. Highway 260 from Holbrook, cut through Petrified Forest and over U.S. 66 through Gallup, Indian trading center, and on to Albuquerque. You can reach Santa Fe that night.

Seventh Day: There is much to see in Santa Fe, but you should leave before noon. A brief side trip to San Ildefonso Pueblo will get you to Taos in time for a short but interesting afternoon there.

TWO WEEKS IN SUMMER (generally north)

One day: From Albuquerque to Santa Fe, thence to Taos Pueblo.
Two days: Great Sand Dunes Nat. Mon.; Mesa Verde Nat. Park.
Two days: Arches Nat. Mon. and Capitol Reef Nat. Mon.
Two days: Bryce Canyon Nat. Park, Cedar Breaks Nat. Mon.
One day: Zion Nat. Park, St. George, and Utah's cotton area.
Two days: Pipe Spring Nat. Mon. to North Rim Grand Canyon.
One day: Wupatki Nat. Mon., Flagstaff and vicinity.
One day: Meteor Crater, Petrified Forest, Gallup, and Albuquerque.

TWO WEEKS IN WINTER (generally south)

(Reverse route if you come from the west):
One day: Big Bend Nat. Park. Next day via old Fort Davis to—
Two days: Carlsbad Caverns Nat. Park. Via Artesia and Cloudcroft to White Sands Nat. Mon., and on to—
One day: El Paso, Tex., and Juárez, Mexico. Via U.S. 80 to—
Two days: Tucson, Ariz., and Saguaro Nat. Mon., Tumacacori Nat. Mon., San Xavier Mission, and Arizona-Sonora Desert Museum.
Two days: Organ Pipe Cactus Nat. Mon., Gulf of Calif., and thence to Phoenix.
One day: To Flagstaff via Jerome, Montezuma Castle and Well.
Two days: Via Wupatki Nat. Mon. to South Rim Grand Canyon.
One day: Hoover Dam and Lake Mead Nat. Rec. Area.
Two days: Las Vegas, Nev., and Death Valley Nat. Mon., Joshua Tree Nat. Mon., and other attractions of SE California.

A 3-WEEK TOUR OF THE SOUTHWEST This tour of the whole Southwest is best taken in either April or October to avoid temperature extremes. If you must visit the Southwest in summer or in winter, expand one of the trips outlined on p. 15 to fit your schedule. By avoiding the peak of either season, you will miss the crowds and enjoy the country more.

One day: Big Bend Nat. Park, Tex.

Two days: Carlsbad Caverns Nat. Park, White Sands Nat. Mon., El Paso, and Juárez, Mex.

Three days: Tombstone; Tucson; Saguaro, Tumacacori, Chiricahua, and Tonto Nat. Mons.; Phoenix; Organ Pipe Cactus Nat. Mon. Then northwestward—

Two days: To Death Valley Nat. Mon., Las Vegas, Lake Mead, and Hoover Dam.

Two days: To Grand Canyon. Visit both rims if you have time.

Three days: Via Pipe Spring Nat. Mon. and Utah's Dixie to Zion and Bryce Canyons and Cedar Breaks Nat. Mon. Try the dirt road over Boulder Mountain and Capitol Reef Nat. Mon. to Natural Bridges and Arches Nat. Mons. Thence to—

Two days: Grand Junction, Colorado Nat. Mon., Black Canyon of the Gunnison, and via Ouray and Silverton (Million Dollar Highway) to Mesa Verde Nat. Park.

Three days: Either through Monument Valley or through the gas and oil country of NW New Mex. to the Indian (Navajo and Hopi) reservations of NE Arizona, Petrified Forest, and Gallup.

Three days: East on U.S. 66 to the Rio Grande Valley of N New Mex., including Albuquerque, Santa Fe, Taos, and the Indian pueblos and picturesque Spanish-American villages and farms.

ADMISSION AND GUIDE FEES are charged by private and, in some cases, federal and state organizations. Religious agencies may invite offerings. Some national parks and monuments charge fees. Most Indian pueblos charge no visiting fee; some do if pictures are taken.

INDIANS OF
THE SOUTHWEST

Man originated in Asia and probably came to North America over a Bering Strait land bridge in many distinct migrations. Some of the migrants, settling in the Southwest, took up life in caves and hunted animals 25,000 or more years ago. By 10,000 years ago, several distinct groups had come or developed; some were hunters,

**Familiar Picture—
Navajo and Burro**

some primitive farmers. Very little is known of man in the Southwest before the beginning of the Christian era. But people living soon after that left their skeletons, tools, and craft work in graves and trash heaps. Study of these remains and dating of them by tree rings and radioactive carbon have enabled scientists to trace several early cultures down to modern Indian groups.

Coronado's arrival in 1540 opened the historic period of Southwestern Indian life and began the long conflict which finally placed Indian tribes on reservations. Today, these picturesque people are citizens. They are being encouraged to expand their colorful arts, customs, and ceremonies and, at the same time, to find a place in today's economy so that they may raise their living standards and have a fair share of opportunity in the Atomic Age.

For more about Indians, read:

PREHISTORIC INDIANS OF THE SOUTHWEST, Wormington, Bull. No. 7, Colo. Mus. Nat. Hist., Denver, 1947.

SOUTHWESTERN ARCHEOLOGY, McGregor, John Wiley & Sons, N. Y., 1941.

MASKED GODS, Frank Waters, Univ. of N. Mex. Press, Albuquerque 1950.

HERE COME THE NAVAHO, Underhill, U. S. Indian Service, Haskell Inst., Lawrence, Kan., 1953.

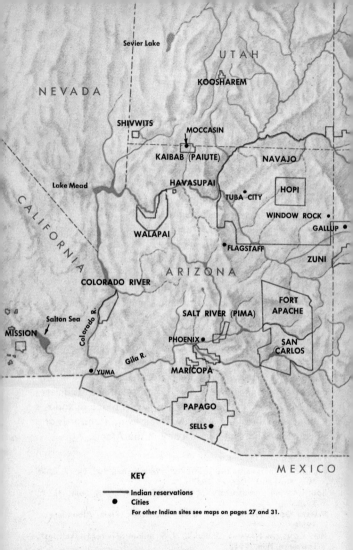

Sevier Lake

UTAH

NEVADA

KOOSHAREM

SHIVWITS

MOCCASIN

KAIBAB (PAIUTE)

NAVAJO

Lake Mead

HAVASUPAI

TUBA CITY

HOPI

WINDOW ROCK

GALLUP

CALIFORNIA

WALAPAI

FLAGSTAFF

ZUNI

ARIZONA

COLORADO RIVER

FORT APACHE

Salton Sea

SALT RIVER (PIMA)

MISSION

PHOENIX

SAN CARLOS

Colorado R.

Gila R.

YUMA

MARICOPA

PAPAGO

SELLS

MEXICO

KEY

Indian reservations

• Cities

For other Indian sites see maps on pages 27 and 31.

18 INDIAN RESERVATIONS

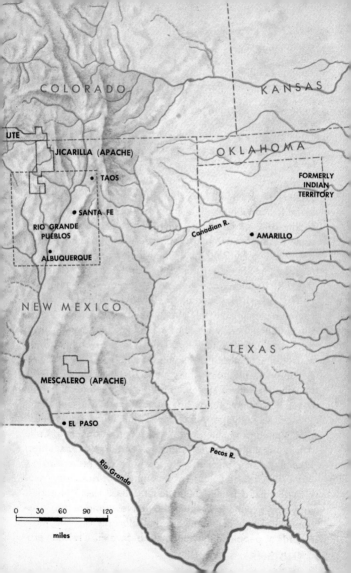

Sandia

Folsom

San Jon

Yuma

EARLIEST INHABITANTS Spear points of flaked stone found with bones of long-extinct bison, camel, mastodon, and mammoth in a cave in the Sandia Mountains near Albuquerque (AL-bu-KER-kee), N. Mex., have been estimated to be 25,000 years old. This earliest record of man in the Southwest has been named the Sandia (san-DEE-ah) Culture. Most famous of the ancient cultures is called Folsom because of finely flaked projectile points found near Folsom, N. Mex., with bones of an extinct bison. Other evidence shows that Folsom people lived between 10,000 and 25,000 years ago. Another group of people, at about the same time, made thick, square-based projectile points, first found near San Jon (HONE), N. Mex. A recent skeletal discovery, older than Folsom Man, in western Texas has been named Midland Man.

More recently, people of the Yuma Culture made beautiful, flaked projectile points, first found near Yuma, Colo. Ancient grinding stones found in Ventana Cave, south of Phoenix, Ariz., and also in southwestern New Mexico, mark the Cochise Culture of fruit-and-root-gathering people who lived from 10,000 to 500 B.C. These materials and others found in Gypsum Cave, Nev., and in the Tabeguache Valley of southwestern Colorado are the main records of people in the Southwest before the Christian era.

ANASAZI CULTURE Anasazi (Navajo for "ancient ones") is the name given to the people who lived over all the plateaulands of the northern Southwest in pre-Christian times. Later raiders, disease, or the great drouth (1276-1299 A.D.) forced them to seek new homes, which their descendants, the Pueblo Indians, now occupy. The early Anasazi were called Basketmakers because of basketry remains found in their caves. These people were semi-agricultural; they built slab-lined storage pits, hunted with spear throwers called atlatls, had dogs, wove clothing from skins and plant fibers, and buried food and equipment with their dead to provide for a future life.

By 500-600 A.D. these people had established communities and had learned how to build pithouse shelters. Another important advance was the start of pottery making. Turkeys may have been domesticated during this time. Beans were added to the crops of corn and squash, and the bow and arrow first came into use. By 800 A.D. the beginnings of modern Pueblo Culture were evident.

**14th Century Hohokam Watchtower (restored) and Irrigation
Canal at Casa Grande National Monument (see p. 136)**

HOHOKAM, MOGOLLON, PATAYAN
While the Anasazi were laying the foundations of the future Pueblo civilization, several cultures developed in southern deserts and valleys. The Hohokam (ho-ho-KAM, Pima for "those who have gone") were farmers who developed an advanced system of irrigation. Shell jewelry, cremation of the dead, finely woven cotton fabrics, and wattle-and-daub houses marked their culture. Hohokam may have been ancestors of the modern Pimas and Papagos. Less is known of the Mogollon (muggy-OHN) Culture, which developed (possibly from the earlier Cochise) in the southern New Mexico-Arizona area. Yuman and Patayan (Walapai for "the old people") groups occupied the Colorado River Valley below Grand Canyon. Knowledge of other groups is scant; few remains have been found. While scientists are still searching, visitors should not do unscientific digging and illegal "pothunting" lest evidence be destroyed which is essential in historical research.

RISE OF PUEBLOS Transition, about 700-800 A.D., from Basketmaker to Pueblo is recognized by the development of many-roomed masonry houses and the modification of the old pithouse to a ceremonial chamber or kiva (KEE-vah). Crude stone hoes and axes came into use. Cotton was a new crop, and the loom was developed. The one-story 6- to 14-room houses were built in a double tier or single row, sometimes L- or U-shaped. Pottery developed with variety in form and decoration. Baskets were still made, but pottery took over many uses. New techniques and materials in weaving appeared. The bow and arrow came into general use. Human bodies were buried, in flexed position, in abandoned storage pits or trash heaps, with pottery and other offerings. Anasazi influence spread, evidence of it being found from the Big Bend area in Texas to southeastern Nevada. By 1000 A.D. nearly all Pueblo traits were established and the stage was set for a great Southwest native civilization to burst into bloom.

Typical House—Early Pueblo Period

Cliff Dwellings at Mesa Verde, Colo.

GOLDEN AGE OF PUEBLOS Pueblo Culture reached its peak in the Southwest while the shadow of the Dark Ages lay over Europe. About 1050 A.D. there was a trend toward great, terraced, communal dwellings several stories high, housing hundreds of people. These were built in the open or under protecting cliffs, as at Mesa Verde National Park, Colo. Much local variation in architecture and in the arts and crafts developed. Pottery was made with a richness of form and design. High-quality cotton cloth reflected progress in weaving, and beautiful turquoise jewelry was made. Dry farming, flood-water farming, and irrigation were practiced.

The end of the golden age began before 1300 A.D. Communal dwellings were gradually abandoned until the entire northern area was deserted. No one knows what caused the emigration — perhaps epidemics, attacks by plundering Navajos and Apaches, destruction of farm land by erosion, internal discord, or famine resulting from the great drouth of 1276-1299. At any rate the works of centuries were abandoned and the people moved to places where conditions were more favorable and where we find their descendants today.

ARTS AND CRAFTS OF THE GOLDEN AGE

Arrowheads

Pottery

Turquoise Beads

Tools

Baskets

Rock Pictures

Taos Pueblo

MODERN PUEBLOS   After the great communal dwellings were abandoned and new villages established, the rejuvenated Anasazi might have risen to a new cultural peak but for the arrival of Europeans in 1540. The Spanish exploring the Southwest found more than 70 inhabited Indian pueblos (in 1955 there were only 30). After the Spanish came, the Indians absorbed new ideas and adopted new materials including metals and livestock. In 1680 the Pueblos revolted and for 12 years were free of Spanish rule. Even today, after long domination by people of European origin, the Pueblos hold to much of their old way of life. Except for the Zuni and Hopi villages, modern Pueblos are in the Rio Grande or tributary valleys. The Indians farm irrigated lands, raise cattle, or work at a variety of jobs. Government and private agencies stimulate continuation of native arts and crafts, and many products find a tourist market. Dances and ceremonials are still practiced as religious or social observances. Visitors are welcome to the villages and to the public dances.

For more about Pueblo Indians, read New Mexico Indians, Bertha P. Dutton, New Mexico Assoc. on Indian Affairs, Santa Fe, N. Mex., 1951, and The Workaday Life of the Pueblo Indians, Underhill, U.S. Indian Service, Haskell Inst., Lawrence, Kan., 1946.

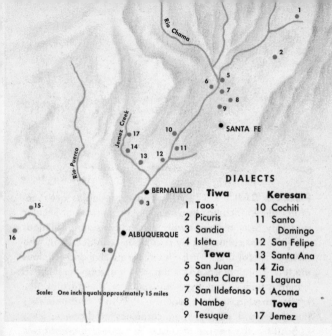

DIALECTS

Tiwa
1 Taos
2 Picuris
3 Sandia
4 Isleta

Tewa
5 San Juan
6 Santa Clara
7 San Ildefonso
8 Nambe
9 Tesuque

Keresan
10 Cochiti
11 Santo Domingo
12 San Felipe
13 Santa Ana
14 Zia
15 Laguna
16 Acoma

Towa
17 Jemez

Scale: One inch equals approximately 15 miles

RIO GRANDE PUEBLOS   The upper Rio Grande Valley has remains of ancient cultures, modern Indian villages, Spanish-speaking towns, up-to-date cities, and workshops of the atom scientists. Pueblo Indian farmers use modern methods of agriculture, tools, and machinery. The homes of these people are a mixture of the ancient and the modern. They use store clothing for daily wear, but the older women still favor native styles for dress-up occasions. Nominally Christianized, the people retain many religious beliefs of their forefathers. Each family has its ceremonial costumes or has custody of communal religious regalia, which is a cherished responsibility. Many Pueblo Indians speak three languages: their own tribal dialect (noted above), Spanish, and English.

Taos War Dance

PUEBLO DAILY LIFE Although the pueblos are generally alike, each has its own social organization. Secular authority rests in an annually elected governor. Religious activities are controlled by a *cacique* (kah-SEE-kee), who holds office for life. *Principáles* integrate civil and religious matters. Religion, based on the idea that man must live in harmony with nature, transcends all else. It integrates arts, crafts, farming, hunting, and social affairs, and underlies Pueblo legend, poetry, song, ceremony, and dance.

Socially, the people of a pueblo belong to one of two kinship groups, each having several kiva or "church" societies. There is also a kachina, or rain-making, cult. A few pueblos do not permit outsiders to view their masked dances, which are often the final and public performances of sacred rites that have been going on for days. If you are able to see a dance, do not take photographs or make sketches or notes unless you have the specific permission of the pueblo governor. Each pueblo holds a fiesta at a fixed date in honor of its patron saint—a Spanish custom. Early priests gave the name of an appropriate saint to each native ceremonial, to direct the rite into reverence for a Catholic patron. (See p. 13.)

Eagle Dancer

28

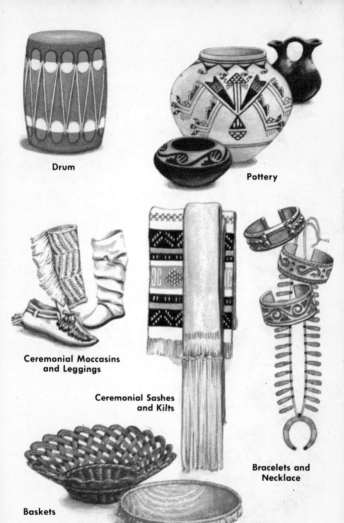

Drum

Pottery

Ceremonial Moccasins
and Leggings

Ceremonial Sashes
and Kilts

Bracelets and
Necklace

Baskets

MODERN RIO GRANDE PUEBLO CRAFT WORK

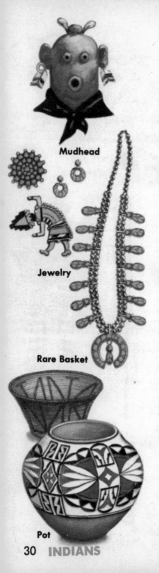

Mudhead

Jewelry

Rare Basket

Pot

THE ZUNIS

Thirty-two miles south of Gallup in the largest pueblo in New Mexico live the Zuni (ZOO-nee) people. Of the 20 known village sites, only 7 were inhabited in 1539, when Estevan-the-Moor became the first European to find and be killed by Puebloans. The next year Coronado captured the Zuni village of Hawiku, but, finding no gold, he continued eastward. After 1706 only one Zuni village was occupied. 3 Zuni villages remained.

Zunis are farmers noted for their pottery and turquoise inlay jewelry. From Europeans they learned to work iron, turning to brass and copper about 1840-1850. By 1870 they had adopted silversmithing and had learned the use of stamps and dies from Navajos. About 1890 they began to develop original techniques that led to exquisite inlay work, which they have been doing ever since. The famous Zuni Shalako ceremony held in November or December each year has become a gathering point for students, visitors, and friends of the Indians of all the Southwest.

Hopi Silver Belt

THE HOPIS On the three Hopi (HO-pee) mesas, at the heart of the Navajo Reservation, are nine villages, discovered by Cárdenas (one of Coronado's lieutenants) in 1540. Oraibi is probably one of the two oldest continuously occupied towns in the United States (Acoma, p. 139, is the other). The Hopis though friendly have long resisted European domination. The Spanish tried to convert them, but in 1680 the Hopis uprose with other Pueblo groups, killed the priests, and destroyed the missions. They were never reconquered. Hopi civil officials are also religious leaders. The household centers around the mother and is the pivot of the village religious and social life. The Hopi seek bountiful crops through intricate ceremonies. Snake dances, held each August as a plea for rain, attract hundreds of visitors. Hopi women make beautiful pottery and baskets. Men carve kachina dolls and weave ceremonial garments.

Powamui Kachina

Black Ogre Kachina

First Mesa

Third Mesa

Second Mesa

First Mesa	Second Mesa	Third Mesa
1 Walpi	4 Mishongnovi	7 Oraibi
2 Sichomovi	5 Shipaulovi	8 Hotevilla
3 Hano	6 Shungopovi	9 Bacabi

To Tuba City
Third Mesa
Second Mesa
First Mesa
To Winslow

YUMAS AND PAIUTES About 14 Yuman tribes called Rancheria (farmer) Indians occupy the lower Colorado River Valley, the hottest part of the Southwest. Besides farming, they hunt, fish, gather wild fruits, and raise cattle. Northernmost of this group, the Paiutes, or Digger Indians, live where Utah, Nevada, and Arizona meet and in nearby California. The Havasupais, living in a canyon that leads into Grand Canyon, and the Walapai, their neighbors to the west, farm and raise cattle. Below Needles, Calif., are the Chemehuevis, who, like the Cocopahs near Yuma, are indifferent agriculturists. Mohaves, in the early days, sometimes settled group differences in individual combat with clubs of mesquite wood. Yumas and Mohaves constantly resisted newcomers of European origin. Many of the Yuman tribes grew native cotton, which women spun and men wove into cloth.

Yuman Woman Spinning

Harvesting Saguaro Fruit

PIMAS AND PAPAGOS Papagos (Desert People) and Pimas (River People) are related tribes of northern Mexico and southern Arizona. Both are farmers, augmenting their crops with cactus fruits, seeds of mesquite and other wild plants, native vegetables, and wild game. Modern Pimas have added wheat and alfalfa to their ancient crops of corn, beans, squash, cotton, and tobacco. Lacking irrigation water, Papagos raise cattle and depend heavily upon native food plants, such as the fruits of the Giant Cactus, the harvest season for which sets the tribal new year. People of both tribes live in small villages (see p. 139). They were friendly to the early Spanish and other settlers, serving as scouts in the Apache campaigns. Both tribes once made pottery for home use, now make beautiful baskets for the tourist trade.

THE UTES, most warlike tribe on the Colorado-Utah plateau, were little known before Escalante's journey through their territory in 1776. The Utes raided pueblos and Spanish settlements until Chief Ouray (yoo-RAY) made peace in 1879. Recent gas and oil developments on their lands have given the Utes new wealth.

THE KIOWAS, now settled in western Oklahoma, once were among the most feared Plains Indians. Joining forces with the Comanches in 1790, they together fought the invaders of their hunting grounds until forced to sign a treaty (later broken) with the United States in 1865.

THE COMANCHES, lords of the southern plains, ranged east of the Rockies and west to the Rio Grande. They fought the Apaches and traded with the Puebloans. These most skillful of Indian horsemen alternated buffalo hunts with raids into Mexico and attacks on wagon trains traveling the Santa Fe Trail. They were suppressed in 1875.

Kiowa Raiding Party

**Apache
Fire Dance**

THE APACHES Apaches are believed to have drifted south from northwestern Canada about 1200-1400 A.D. They were hunters and plant gatherers until the acquisition of Spanish horses remade their way of life. The Apaches hunted buffalo, fought the Comanches (who defeated them in 1723), and raided the pueblos. A scourge to travelers, desert farmer Indians, and Spanish settlements for nearly two centuries, they were finally subdued by the United States Army. Geronimo (her-ON-e-moh) and his band were the last to surrender, in 1886. Now the Apaches, of which there are several tribal groups, are excellent stockmen. Their rituals have never been much publicized, the best known being the annual Gahan Ceremonial at Mescalero, N. Mex., July 1-4. The Apache Fire Dance and the Devil Dance are among the spectacular presentations each August at the Inter-Tribal Ceremonial at Gallup, N. Mex.

Navajo Sand Painting

THE NAVAJOS   The 70,000 Navajos, on their 24,000-square-mile reservation in Arizona, New Mexico, and Utah, form the largest Indian tribe in the U.S. Their forebears drifted down from Northwest Canada about 1200-1400 A.D. First called Apaches by the Spanish, later designated *Apaches de Nabahu'u* (enemies from farmed lands), they finally became known as Navajos. Wandering hunters and plant gatherers, Navajos preferred to raid the fields of the Pueblos. When, in 1848, the United States obtained the Southwest from Mexico, Kit Carson was commissioned to subdue the Navajos. After destroying their sheep and crops, he rounded up 8,000 of the people and in 1864 moved them to Fort Sumner, N. Mex., as prisoners of war. In 1868 the Navajos signed a peace treaty and returned home. Within 10 years they were established again, and by 1934 their sheep and horses had overgrazed the entire reservation and the people were threatened with famine. Now, with the help of oil and uranium royalties, schools, and irrigated farms, the Navajo leaders are working out a tribal program to make their people self-sufficient.

NAVAJO ARTS AND CUSTOMS   Returning from Fort Sumner in 1868, some Navajos undertook farming, but most raised sheep. Flocks and crops are owned by women. The wife is the center of the family; the children are hers and members of her clan. Women and children herd and butcher the sheep, spin the wool, and weave rugs, which are exchanged for clothing, coffee, sugar, or canned foods. Women and children still dress in 1860 styles, wearing long, full, calico skirts and colorful velveteen blouses. Men retain their pride in horsemanship and their wealth in horses. Many men now work for wages. Previously, silversmithing was important men's work. With crude tools and silver dollars or Mexican pesos, Navajo men developed the heavy silver jewelry for which the tribe is famous. Now they use silver slugs or wire to make rings, bracelets, pins, buckles, necklaces, and concho belts. Men represent their families at ceremonies and in public. All rituals have a definite objective: to secure food, insure survival, regain health, or cast out evil spirits. These rites, called "sings," are important also as social gatherings.

Navajo Silversmith

37

Navajo Loom and Hogan

NAVAJO WEAVING   Navajo families in winter live in dome-shaped hogans made of logs or stones and earth. In summer, when they are on the move searching for grass for the sheep, they build a simple brush shelter wherever they stay for a few days. Here the wife does housekeeping and sets up her loom, weaving rugs when time permits. All members of the family help with shearing, but the children watch the sheep and the women wash, card, spin, and dye the wool. Navajos learned weaving from the Pueblos and, soon after obtaining sheep from the Spanish, began weaving blankets, using their own wool and native dyes. With twisted yarns and commercial dyes, new designs came. Navajos prefer lighter, more colorful Pendleton wool blankets; so, after 1890, they began to make rugs for sale. In recent years weaving has declined.

For more about Navajos and Apaches read:

TRADERS TO THE NAVAHO, Wetherill, Univ. of N. Mex. Press, Albuquerque, 1952.

APACHE AGENT, Clum, Houghton Mifflin Co., Boston, 1936.

NAVAHO SHEPHERD AND WEAVER, Gladys Amanda Reichard, J. J. Augustin, Locust Valley, L. I., N. Y., 1936.

APACHE DAYS AND AFTER, Criese, Caxton Printers, Caldwell, Ida., 1941.

NAVAHO WEAVING, Amsden, Univ. of N. Mex. Press, Albuquerque, 1949.

THE NAVAHO, Kluckhohn and Leighton, Harvard Univ. Press, Cambridge, Mass., 1947.

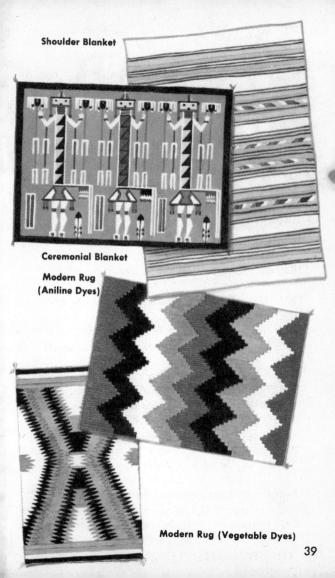

Shoulder Blanket

Ceremonial Blanket

Modern Rug
(Aniline Dyes)

Modern Rug (Vegetable Dyes)

HISTORICAL TIMETABLE

1276-99: Long drouth forces Indians to seek new homes.

1536: Cabeza de Vaca crosses Southwest en route to New Spain.

1540-42: Coronado explores Southwest from Grand Canyon to Kansas.

1581-1600: Many Spanish expeditions follow Coronado.

1598: Juan de Oñate sets up first capital at San Juan.

1610: New capital at Santa Fe, terminus of Mexican route.

1680: Pueblo Indians revolt and drive out Spanish.

1692: De Vargas recaptures SW. Father Kino develops chain of missions among Pima and Papago Indians.

1776: Escalante explores present W Colorado and Utah.

1803: Louisiana Purchase brings United States into SW.

1813: Old Spanish Trail partly follows Escalante's route.

1822: Mexico wins independence from Spain.

1824: U.S. trappers push into SW from east and north.

1830-31: Old Spanish Trail extended to California.

1833: Vein gold discovered in New Mexico.

1844: Fremont explores Utah and Colorado until 1853.

1846: Texas joins U.S. as 28th state. War with Mexico!

1847: Mormons settle Utah and open wagon route from Santa Fe to California.

1848: Mexican War ends. SW transferred to U.S. with boundary along Rio Grande and Gila River.

1849: Stages begin operation over the Santa Fe Trail. Gold rush brings deaths along Camino del Diablo.

1850: U.S. buys "Santa Fe County" from Texas.

1853: Gadsden Purchase sets final Mexican boundary.

1854-56: Silver mining reaches a new high in Arizona.

1857-59: Beale through SW with camels. Pikes Peak gold rush.

1862: Civil War splits SW. Texans invade New Mexico.

1860-1890: Mormons from Utah colonize Arizona.

1864: Navajos defeated by Kit Carson, moved to Ft. Sumner.

1866: Nevada joins Union as 36th state.

1869: Powell's boats conquer Colorado River in Grand Canyon.

873: Crook subdues Tontos, Yavapaís and Walapais.

1876: Coal mining started in Utah. Barbed wire ends epoch of open range. Colorado becomes 38th state.

1877-78: Tombstone and Bisbee—mining boom towns.

1881: SW connected to Pacific Coast by railroad.

1886: Geronimo surrenders, ending Indian resistance.

1896: Utah becomes 45th state.

MT. WHEELER +

Sevier Lake

GRAND JUNCT

MOAB

NEVADA

UTAH

CALIENTE

Colorado R.

LEEDS

San Juan R.

BEATTY

Old Spanish Trail

ST. GEORGE

MT. TRUMBULL +

Grand Canyon

DEATH VALLEY

FT. DEFIANCE

Lake Mead

PAINTED DESERT

FT. WINGATE

MOJAVE DESERT

SEARCHLIGHT

FLAGSTAFF

CALIFORNIA

Havasu Lake

JEROME

FT. WHIPPLE

SAN BERNARDINO MTS.

INDIO

ARIZONA

Colorado R.

Coronado's Route

Salton Sea

Gila R.

PHOENIX

SILVER

Mormon Battalion

SILVER KING

FT. GRANT

SHAKESPEARE

TUCSON

FT. BOWIE

FT. LOWELL

TUBAC

TOMBSTONE

MEXICO

KEY

– – – – Mormon Battalion
─────── Santa Fe Trail
+++++++ Goodnight-Loving Cattle Drive
━ ━ ━ ━ Escalante's Route
· · · · · Coronado's Route
– – – – Old Spanish Trail
+++++++ Chihuahuan Highway
–·–·–·– Butterfield's Stagecoach Route, 1857-61
● Cities
□ Old Forts
○ Ghost Towns

For Indian features see maps on pages 18-19, 27, and 31.